Lyman Whitney Allen

Abraham Lincoln

A Poem

Lyman Whitney Allen

Abraham Lincoln
A Poem

ISBN/EAN: 9783744708883

Printed in Europe, USA, Canada, Australia, Japan

Cover: Foto ©Thomas Meinert / pixelio.de

More available books at **www.hansebooks.com**

ABRAHAM LINCOLN

A POEM

BY

LYMAN WHITNEY ALLEN

G. P. PUTNAM'S SONS

NEW YORK
27 West Twenty-third Street

LONDON
24 Bedford Street, Strand

The Knickerbocker Press

1896

The Knickerbocker Press, New York

This book is a revised edition of the prize poem, "Abraham Lincoln," published in *The New York Herald*, December 15th, 1895.

CONTENTS.

Invocation.

INVOCATION.

OF one great Ship that sailed the sea
  And weathered the infuriate blast ;
  Of one great Pilot that stood fast
And brought her into lee,

I sing ; and singing seek to use
  Thy founts of grace, as they of yore
  Sought and found service in thy store,
O immemorial Muse !

3

The Grecian Poet, quaffing thence
  Castalian cheer, song's classic lord
  Awoke the mythic centuried chord
Of life's diviner sense.

The Florentine with screenèd eyes
  Caught rich and Beatrician gleam
  Of Eunoë's redemptive stream
And beams of Paradise.

The Seer of Horton, finding meet
  Thy rills beyond the hills of time,
  Set primal sorrow into rhyme,
And sin to music sweet.

INVOCATION.

The Laureate of the Holy Grail,
   Deep-drinking, placed before thy face
   The Idyll-Epic of the race,
The quest's supreme avail.

The Cambridge Singer o'er the walls
   Of custom clomb, and roaming found,
   On far Itascan storied ground,
The Laughing Water Falls;

The twilight of primeval pines,
   The leafy homes of plumèd quires,
   Mondamin's green and golden spires,
And Hiawatha's shrines.

O ancient Muse forever young !
   Guard of the poets' mystic spring !
   Touch heart and tongue that I may sing
Somewhat as they have sung,—

One simple strain of that great song,
   Which ardent bards through future years,
   O'er ever-brightening hemispheres,
Shall rapturously prolong ;

Sweet burthen since the world began,
   Desire of every century,
   Imperious Love's sublime decree,—
The brotherhood of man.

THE HEART OF FREEDOM.

THE fragrant meadows of Runnymede
   Grow greener with every succeeding year ;
The Ironside hoofs of the Puritan's steed
   Still crowd on the Cavalier.

The laurel blooms upon Burial Hill ;
   The broken tablets are slabs of gold ;
And Plymouth Rock in the winter's chill
   With summer is aureoled.

The thunders of Concord and Lexington
    Roll on in music that will not die;
And one brave venture for Freedom done
    Immortally crowns July.

White stars of dawn in a sky of blue,
    And bars of glory o'er land and sea,
Shall float the emblem all ages through
    Of Union and Liberty.

So stands our hope with its blessings spread,
    A magna charta inviolate;
The deathless soul of the patriot dead;
    The heart of the living State.

SHIPS OF FATE.

Two paths apart on the misty main ;
 Two eager prows toward the beaconing West ;
O'er crests of courage, through troughs of pain,
 Of life and of death possessed.

Above the one from seraphic wings
 Blew friendly winds 'gainst the crowded sails ;
And fingers used to celestial strings
 Held back on the rushing gales.

9

Below the other a rising sweep
  Of forms foam-raimented; raven hands
Forced fiercely through the resentful deep
  Swift woe unto western lands.

Fair *Mayflower*, breasting the wintry sea!
  Thou wert the promise of wakening spring;
Embosoming Freedom's destiny
  And Liberty's issuing.

Dark Slaver, touching Virginia's shore!
  With captives laden from mast to keel;
Thou wert the sign of the deepening sore
  Of wrong that could only heal

SHIPS OF FATE.

In smoke of battle and streams of blood,

In orphan cries unto winds and waves,

In tears of precipitate widowhood

Bedewing a million graves.

A Dream of Empire.

13

A DREAM OF EMPIRE.

A FRUITFUL land 'neath Southern skies,
  With verdant fields and blossomed meads;
And o'er the seas increasing rise
  The cries of Europe's greatening needs.

Wide-stretching belts of meltless snows
  Through swarms of swarthy forms displayed;
And purple wealth to golden grows
  Along the thoroughfares of trade.

15

A dream of empire such as ne'er

    Glowed on the vision of the race;

A bounteous breadth of tropic sphere,

    A luminous ocean-rounded space,

From Hatteras to Panama,

    And summer shores of Mazatlan,

To copper hills of Arriba

    Beyond the bays of Yucatan;

And on o'er Amazonian plain,

    Past Pampean sea and jewelled bourn,

Through Incan trails and tracks of Spain,

    One empire to the Southern Horn.

An empire with its gilded throne
    By flesh and blood enslavèd wrought ;
An empire with its pillared zone
    Of states, whose founders nobly fought

For right and faith, but failed to trace,
    The while their life-blood stained the sod,
Within the negro's ebon face
    The image of Almighty God.

And later scions holding fast
    Their legacies of sophistry,
Preferred the world's discordant past,
    Forsook the footsteps of the free,

To tread apart revulsive ways,

    Back from the ascending trend of things,

Back toward the nations' yesterdays,

    Hand unto hand again with kings.

The Star of Sangamon.

19

THE STAR OF SANGAMON.

A NATION called through the gloom

In one long wail of despair,

One multitudinous prayer,

'Neath portent of hastening doom ;

And myriad strainèd eyes

Were lifted to lowering skies.

But on a sudden the night

Was shaken : a marvellous light

Burst forth, an effulgent spark

Against the o'erwhelming dark.

It waxed, it whitened, it shone
Aflame in the widening zone
Of dawn ; and a world intent
Read, scanning the firmament,
God's covenant blazed thereon,
America's horoscope,
The sign of a Nation's hope,
The Star of Sangamon.

Not out of the East but the West
A Star and a Savior rose ;
A light to an eager quest,
A spirit of grace possessed,
Of faith 'mid increasing woes,
Of wisdom manifest.

And, forth from the variant past
Of thraldom's darkness, at last
·God's measureless love for man
Wrought through heredity's dower
The great American,
Whose soul was the perfect flower
Of patriot planting in soil
Kept moist by blood and tears,
And fertile by faithful toil
Throughout unnumbered years.

Nor accident nor chance,
But heavenly ordinance
Set his nativity
In ripened fulness of time,

For sake of a race to be
The pledge of a golden prime.

In lowliest spot he breathed
His first sweet breath of the earth ;
And life's great Parent bequeathed
Fair virginal Nature from birth
To be his tutor and friend,
His youthful steps to attend.

She led o'er the wooded hills
And flowering prairied vales,
Along by the summer's rills,
Against the winter's gales,
Through sweeps of primeval ills,
Across the Red Men's trails.

She taught him the songs of birds,

The sympathy-syllabled words

Of water and earth and air,

And pointed the winding stair

That leads to Heaven, where climb

The higher forces of time.

She bound him, that he might feel

The weight of Oppression's heel;

She starved him, that he might learn

The hunger of souls that yearn;

She bruised him, that he might know

Somewhat of the world's great woe.

She helmed him with faith; she placed

The girdle of strength at his waist;

And over his breast she laid
The buckler of right ; the blade
Of truth she set in his hand
And bade him unwavering stand,
As Moses stood with his rod,
For Freedom and God.

At length in a deathless hour
She kissed him ; a quickening power
Shot forth through her lips of fire
In touch of divine desire.

One long sweet look of review ;
Then suddenly from her she threw
Her manifold mantle of mystery ;
And, facing the great Before,

On unto the famèd door

That opens out into history,

In radiant rapture she led

Her hero all panoplied,

And thrust him from her to be,

On mission immortal bent,

Transfigurer of despair,

The champion of Liberty,

The hope of a continent,

God's answer to prayer.

THE PEOPLE'S KING.

NOT oft such marvel the years reveal,
  Such beauteous thing,
  A People's King,
The chosen liege of a chosen weal,
  And Liberty's offering.

Not oft such product the fair world hath,
  A People's Own,
  On mightiest throne,
Whose strong foundations are Right and Faith,
  And Virtue the corner-stone.

Not by earth's bounty was he prepared ;
　　Not princely store,
　　Nor golden lore,
Was nurture on which his nature fared
　　For strength in the trust he bore ;

But inner largess of revenue,
　　Past time and space,
　　The fruits of grace,
That mellowed upon the tree which grew
　　God's food for a famished race.

In history's mirror he truly saw
　　The ages' strife,

With passion rife,

'Neath covenant promise a changeless law

Writ clear in its serial life.

He learned from the centuries' battle-fields

What heroes are,

How maim and scar

Are gloried trophies to him who yields

Himself to the shocks of war;

That patriot sires have taught their sons,

Since days of eld,

How Truth is held,

And Justice fashions a nation's guns

Never to be repelled.

Thus was it a purpose for valiant deeds,
　Like whitening flame,
　Through all his frame
Swept burning until his Country's needs
　His one great thought became.

Thus was it he took in his sovereign hand,
　With face to Fate,
　The orb of state,
To serve his Country and God, and stand
　To them all consecrate.

Fort Sumter.

33

FORT SUMTER.

O'ER sea-girt fortress set toward Charleston's
  orient sun
  Columbia's banner waved, and 'neath it, in
  array,
  A noble band stood waiting for the break of
  day,
And Southland's primal gun.

Soon from Palmetto shores and isles historic
  burst
  War's first unfilial thunder, and a signal shell

Rose   screaming   seaward   over   guardian
        citadel,
Predestined and accurst.

An omened silence; then from bastioned shoals
        of ire,
    Raged, blazing under wide and reddened fir-
        mament,
    One hurricane of havoc into swift descent
Of fierce columbiad fire.

Guns answered guns, till thrice from morn to
        eventide
    The worn defenders strove behind embat-
        tered bars,

And faithful to their Country's hallowed
    Stripes and Stars
Rebellion's host defied.

At length, within shot-swept and ravaged ram-
    parts, broke
Mad conflagration, driven 'neath furious can-
    nonade,
As if the traitorous Earth had molten wrath
    displayed
Hurled through volcanian smoke.

Before resistless storm the standard fell, but
    leapt
Aloft mid clouds enfuming, and in proud
    disdain

Streamed from its splintered staff above the
    wreck and pain
And vows of soldiers kept.

Thrust forth by flame and Fate, all honored
    in retreat,
    They unsurrendering went, their banner
        holding fast
    To float thereon again, redeemed, and be at
        last
Their leader's winding-sheet.

The die was cast; Secession's deed flashed to
    renown ;
    The golden South had drunk of her self-
        poisoned cup ;

And swift a loyal People's slumberous blood
    rose up
When Sumter's flag went down.

And one, a Nation's Prophet, with sad eyes
    afar
  Beholding, steadfast gazed beyond near space
    and time
  Upon the advancing tide, and saw it sweep
    sublime
The purple paths of war.

COLUMBIA'S WRATH.

THE guns that fired on Sumter's walls
    Awoke a Nation ; far and near
    Were cries of anguish, bursts of fear
And burning judgment calls.

Beloved Columbia, wounded sore,
    A moment staggered ; then her form
    Rose towering, while a gathering storm
Her darkening features wore.

40

Her flag that waved o'er Southern sea
   Had fallen while she slept ; but now
   The cloud upon her bended brow
Was certain augury

Of hastening vengeance, and the fire,
   That flashed from all her kindled tips
   Of being, was apocalypse
Of purpose swift and dire ;

Of purpose dire until the Right
   In dust and blood should conquer Wrong;
   Till mists should lift and morning's song
Sound through the passing night;

Till victor hosts should rise and plant
  That flag on Sumter's height again ;
  And wipe away for aye her stain,
And sign her covenant,

Blood-writ across a million graves,
  That, in her undivided land,
  There nevermore should rest a band
Upon a race of slaves.

The Call to Arms.

THE CALL TO ARMS.

BESIDE Columbia stood one
  Begot of Holy Liberty;
  Exalted by her grace to be
Her favored regnant son.

That sacred trust his heart and brain
  In swift and sweet devotion drew;
  And well his loyal nature knew
The measure of her pain.

And all his being rose with hers;
  Till, facing her intense distress,
  Remembering the faithfulness
Of past deliverers,

He took from out his sacred girth
  The golden trumpet which he bore;
  Blew such a blast as ne'er before
Was heard in all the earth;

A blast that sounded war's alarms,
  From north to south, from east to west;
  Columbia's supreme behest,
The Nation's call to arms.

The People's Response.

THE PEOPLE'S RESPONSE.

IT rang o'er the startled land
One sovereign blast of command.
It rolled from sea unto sea,
The summons of Liberty.
It broke 'gainst the scintillant hills,
Resounding in multiple thrills
Of wakening thunder. It swept
Through valleys and over streams
The militant havoc of dreams
Of troubled millions that slept.
It stirred all hearts as it went,
Arousing a continent.

The People's answer came ;

A splendor burst on the night ;

The crests of the hills were flame ;

The valleys were lines of light ;

The winds were voices of trust ;

A soul was incarnate in dust ;

The frame of the struggling earth

Drew nigh to a larger birth.

The People leapt to their feet,

Their strength like a giant's brawn,

Their zeal like a furnace heat,

Their hope like the widening dawn.

And up to the throne of Him

Who reigns 'twixt the cherubim,

Mid supplicatory throes

A vow inviolate rose;

That, be it through torturing pain,

Their banner should rise again;

That ne'er should the Federal Stars

Give place to the Southern Bars;

That, under God's judgment sky,

Rebellion at last should lie

In overthrow complete

Beneath Columbia's feet.

And thus a People quivering stood

And offered their blood.

The crags replied to the echoing crags,

And flags waved answer to flags.

O'er wharf and harbor, o'er vale and hill,

And loyal domicile,

O'er school and languishing academe

A banner floated supreme.

O'er bustling mart and thoroughfare

One standard streamed to the air.

From argent turrets and glittering spires

The pennons of sainted sires

Were signs of a storied Faith that wore

Her lustrous robes as of yore.

The steam-shod chargers of turbulent trade,

Thundering through meadow and glade,

Were freighted for Freedom, and southward flew

Ablaze with the Red, White and Blue.

And vows were written again and again,

Till earth was a manuscript,

Illuminated by patriot pen
In triplicate glory dipt.

The plow was left in the fallow field
For sake of a larger yield.
The iron lay cold in the smouldering flame
Because of a higher claim.
The rattling shuttle, the whirring loom
Were hushed at the cannon's boom.
And over the land the market's hum
Gave place to the fife and drum.
The workers, trained for the shop and mill,
Aspired to a warrior's skill.
The poet deserted his golden song
To join the armèd throng.

The sculptor forsook his half-carved stone

At sound of the bugle blown.

Each town and hamlet became a spring

Of chivalric issuing,

A living current of sacrifice

Full-set toward a great emprise.

The plowshares sprang into glistening swords,

And pruning-hooks into spears ;

Love's accents broke into farewell words,

And laughter to bitter tears.

Across the threshold the mother gave

Her son for a soldier's grave ;

And freely yielded the weeping wife

The heart of her heart for strife.

Despair strode in through the gates of home,

And Hope fled forth to roam.

All hearts were one, and the Nation's soul

Moved on toward its sacred goal.

Beneath the sky's cerulean hue

The hills and the vales were blue.

The sun flashed down, in its dazzling wheel,

On billows of bristling steel.

THE GATHERING OF THE LEGIONS.

MAJESTIC swept from coast to coast
Columbia's azure-liveried host.
From Pilgrim havens, from Pine-Tree shades,
And over the walls of the Palisades ;
From Eldorado's aureate sand,
Past geyser vales of the Wonderland ;
From linkèd lakes, from the castled mounds
Of Gathering Waters, from forest bounds ;
O'er purple canyons and ferny glens,
Ravined plateaus and miasmal fens,
Meridian rivers and prairies wide,
And granite domes of the Great Divide ;
From Empire Portal, from Golden Gate,

To Country and Liberty consecrate,

With " Union forever " their rallying cry,

To stand for the Colors, or under them die,

By one unfaltering faith controlled,

The patriot legions onward rolled ;

On, on, at the clarion call of him

Who stood with face to a spectre grim,

And saw, o'er the crests of the surging tide,

The crimson Furies of Fratricide ;

On, on, toward the hallowed citadel,

Where Freedom's chosen guardians dwell ;

On, on, the myriads swept along,

With rhythmic tread and with ringing song,

With heralding bugle and fife and drum :

" We come, Father Abraham, we come,

Six hundred thousand strong."

OUR VOLUNTEERS.

O SACRED miracle wrought of truth !

    Of truth and time,

    And love sublime !

And through the bloom of perpetual youth,

    The wonder of every clime !

O summer of sorrow that gloams afar !

    Across the years

    Of mists and tears !

How beauteous now the memories are

    That halo your Volunteers !

O Freemen who rose when their Country called!

    Such patriots those,

    Where else disclose,

Or lands or seasons by Heaven forestalled,

    Against impetuous foes?

Immortal Legions that gathered then!

    When skies were black,

    And Freedom's track

Lay close by chasms which none could ken,

    And under the tempest's wrack!

O Heroes that never shall be forgot!

    Though life be done,

    And rest be won,

And earth be given for blesseder spot
    That needs no light of the sun!

Columbia's power supreme shall last,
    Through endless years,
    Beyond all fears,
The future risen above the past,
    Upheld by her Volunteers.

The Price of Liberty.

61

THE PRICE OF LIBERTY.

THE price of liberty is patriot blood.
Thus is it written with the dripping sword
Across the pages of the ages past.
Where'er uplifted stands the crownèd Good,
Beneath her bleeding feet lies Evil's horde,
Defiant and contending to the last.

So was it that the azure sky of noon
Should darken, and calm Nature terrified
Should tremble in the fierce and thun-
derous jar ;
So was it that the flowered fields of June
Should redden, and æolian summer-tide
Grow strident with the agony of war.

BULL RUN.

LONG lines of steel in the morning,
    Wide winding columns of blue;
        The Sabbath's hush,
        The dawn's sweet flush,
Brave hearts all failure scorning
    And fresh as the glistening dew.

High noon o'er the trampled meadows
    And Bull Run's crimsoned stream;
        Hot shot and shell
        And swaths of Hell;
Bold forms in the flaming shadows
    Aface to a fiery dream.

Dust-clouds in the evening rising,

Fresh hope to a turning foe;

Tumultuous flight,

Blood, rapine and night;

The Nation's heart agonizing,

A clamor of fear and woe.

5

The Nation's Prophet.

67

THE NATION'S PROPHET.

THE hour was come, and with it rose the man
    Ordained of God and fashioned for the hour;
       The savior of a race;
For whom wrought ever, since the world began,
    The subtle energies of thought and power
       In lineal lines of grace.

Incarnate Conscience; Right's embodiment;
    Benignant Nature's generous bequest
       In mind and feature writ;
Life's lore and legends into wisdom blent;
    Past verities to present truth compressed;
       The People's composite.

A master-soul was his that gazing saw
　　The refluent tide of battle, felt the fires
　　　That swept all withering ;
A master-soul, set to a higher law,
　　That heard above the Earth's despairing
　　　quires
　　Of heavenly promise sing.

THE NIGHT OF SORROW.

THE skies withdrew their guidings; star by
    star
    Fled from the circuit of engulfing cloud ;
      The moon eclipsèd glowed
Unbeauteous beyond her lurid bar ;
    And forth, inexpiate and crimson-browed,
      Carnage emblazoned strode.

The midnight deepened, and war's widening
    way
    Shook 'neath his clangorous tread all uncon-
      trolled.

The winds were bruiting breath
Of Consternation laden with red spray ;
    And happenings were spectres that foretold
    Impending doom and death.

And Pain was myriad-throated ; and Despair
    Waxed flagrant with unloosed and vagrant
        tongue ;
    Terror's envenomed pack
Tore at the bosom of scarce-struggling Prayer ;
    Distrust o'er pallid Faith her mantle flung,
    Along war's ghastly track.

THE VIGIL.

AND one beside Columbia's prostrate form
  Watched, in lone vigil, from his regent height
  The Nation's hopes decline ;
And set intrepid breast against the storm,
  Facing the fury of inflamed despite,
  Waiting celestial sign ;

While through the fiery. rifts his worn eyes
    strained
  Past wastes of graves, where hosts, once glis-
    tening,
  Now silent prisoners lay ;

73

And saw with priceless blood the green earth
　　stained,
　And war's low-flying vultures, wing to wing,
　Disaster and Dismay.

Seven times refined by fire, his mediate soul
　　Heard the unburthening and ascending woes
　　Of serried sacrifice,
The anguished sighings of his People, roll
　　Up to the throne of God; and felt the
　　　throes
　　Of supplication rise;

And caught the wailings from expanses higher
　Of multitudes that 'neath the altar cried,
　" How long, O Lord, how long?

How long ere Justice shall her rod acquire?
  How long ere Vengeance forth in might shall
    ride
  Against Earth's hoary wrong?"

And, far uplifted on the slopes of grace,
  His soul, in prayer impassioned, touched
    with God
  Through puissant lengths of faith;
When, lo, before him flashed from farther
    space,
  Cloud-clothed, with rainbowed brow and feet
    fire-shod,
  Above the tempest's path,

His troubled Country's Guardian Hierarch,
    Imperious by Earth's supreme demand
        And Heaven's august decree;
In flaming splendor vanquishing the dark,
    Pointing past duty with directing hand
        Down ways of victory.

THE VOICE OF DESTINY.

THE hour was come, and in that hour he stood
    Responsive to the sacred voice that spake
    From Heaven and earth and sea.
He heard the dusky toiling multitude
    Plaintively pleading that his hand should
       break
    Their bonds and set them free.

He heard the voice of God from shining height,
    Who, for the reason of the Nation's sin,
    Had held her armies back

In failure and defeat, till she should right
  The wrongs herself had sanctioned, and
    should win
  Justice unto her track;

When, girded with the strength of righteous-
    ness,
  God for her, with descending seraphim,
  Above the battle's tide,
She then would march to triumph, and possess
  A land united to the farthest rim,
    Through sorrow purified.

The Stroke of Justice.

79

THE STROKE OF JUSTICE.

THE hour was come, the Nation's crucial hour;
    A crisis of the world, a turn of time;
      The ages' hope and dream.
And one undaunted soul, sinewed with power,
    Freedom's anointed, rose to height sublime,
      Imperial and supreme;

And, lifting high o'er groaning multitude
    His sovereign sceptre, smote with such a
      stroke
      The chains of centuries,

6

That earth was shaken to its farthest rood ;
   That millioned manacles asunder broke,
      And myriad properties

Became, in one immortal moment,—men ;
   Free with the free in all the rounded earth ;
      Redeemed by martyr blood ;
To stand with faces to the light again,
   Attaining through their resurrection birth,
      To human brotherhood.

THE DAWN.

THE shadows slowly lifted from the sun ;
    The benediction splendors downward rolled,
      Fore-flush of day to be;
The Nation's Prophet stood, his mission done,
    Upon the covenant mountains, aureoled
      With immortality.

The shadows slowly lifted, and the Land
    Grew glad, e'en though the blood of heroes
      veined
      Her fair and sacred face ;
For Right at last had risen to command,
    And Justice had in her Republic gained
      Her high and holy place.

The Apotheosis.

85

THE APOTHEOSIS.

To one superior peak, before untrod,
    Alone he clomb, the summons heard by
        naught
        Save his interior soul;
The Nebo of his life, the mount of God
    All luminous; and marvelling he caught
        Swift vision of the goal

Of his unwavering faith, the Promised Land
    Toward which his feet had led his People on
        O'er wastes of blood and fire;
And gazing saw the breadths of grace expand,
    Apocalyptic in the halcyon dawn
        Of centuried desire.

He saw across the lessening hurricane
 His Country's armies march to victory ;
  And, lifted to the light,
The Stars and Stripes in glory wave again,
 Invincible, the standard of the free,
  The sacred sign of right.

He saw the battle-clouds disperse for aye ;
 The camp-fires of the Nation smouldering ;
  A million veterans tread
The smiling paths along the homeward way,
 Expectant gates of welcome open swing,
  And feasts of gladness spread.

The vision widened, and the distant view
  Grew clearer till the fugitive forecast
    Of far horizons shone;
And earth became a throngèd avenue
  With multitudes processional that passed
    Before his prophet throne.

He saw the golden South refashioned rise,
  Transcending all her dreams imperial,
    To greatening power and fame;
A deeper azure in her bending skies,
  Increasing wealth of nature quickening all
    Her strong and beauteous frame.

He saw the argent North anew inspired,
  Beneath her holy chrism, to truer love
    For her rich heritage,
The revenue of sacrifice acquired
  In service, which, from hallowed founts above,
    Shall flow through every age.

He saw the wounds of war in Union healed;
  No North, no South; from sea to mountain
    tip
  One land, one flag for aye;
And kindred blood, mixt on the battle-field,
  Cementing, in perpetual fellowship,
    The Nation's Blue and Gray.

He saw the marble columns 'gainst the sky ;

  The flowered garlands o'er the palls of green ;

    The gathered worshippers

Conning the story that 'tis sweet to die

  For Country, and to win the prize serene

    A grateful world confers.

The splendor spread to its meridian prime,

  And earth lay fruited 'neath the noon's

    caress ;

    He saw from zone to zone

The feet of Love upon the crests of Time,

  The hand of Peace dispensing blessedness

    From Freedom's central throne.

He saw the upward march of centuries ;
    He heard the gloried sweeps of gratitude
    Above the glad earth rise,
Antiphonal with strains of heavenly bliss,
    The diapasons of beatitude,
        Hymnings of Paradise.

Listening, he heard the sweet adagios
    Of quiring angels, and the morning song
    Of the redeemed and free ;
And was not, for God took him ; and he rose
    Caught to the bosom of that martyr throng
    Who died for Liberty.

THE VOICE OF MARTYRDOM.

IN the great world there are no accidents;
    Enthroned above the ages' ebb and flow,
        Unseen, misunderstood,
God rules, who in all seasons and events,
    Through fiery evil and o'erwhelming woe,
        Forever works the good.

And God hath wrought the good; forevermore
    The million-mouthèd cries of martyrdom
        Are one immortal voice,
That sounds triumphant o'er the mighty roar
    Of instant days and centuries to come,
        And bids the world rejoice.

Rejoice that Freedom's gifts the earth adorn,

And every path is open thoroughfare

Won on the fields of strife;

That man may mount to highways of the

morn,

With Faith the light, and Hope the fragrant

air,

And Charity the life.

The Pledge of History.

.

95

THE PLEDGE OF HISTORY.

COLUMBIA, great Mother ; through all lands
   The memory of her storied prowess runs
And glorified expands.
Columbia enfreedomed ; thus she stands,
   Behind the bulwark of her noble sons,
Robed in her starry bands.

Behold her risen from embattled plains,
   More beautiful by all her holy scars
And sacred martial stains !
What grace and wisdom her proud form attains !
   With sheathèd sword beneath her Stripes
      and Stars
How tranquilly she reigns !

7

Her realm is of all realms the goodliest,
　　The fairest of the new Hesperides ;
A zone of fulness blest
With golden fruits unfound in ancient quest,
　　And gladdening wine all sweet unto the lees ;
The free and welcoming West.

She knows the bitter of Oppression's gall ;
　　She knows the taste of Freedom's nectared
　　　　cheer ;
And when the sorrowing call,
E'en though it be beyond her ocean wall,
　　Remembering her past, shall she not hear
And Liberty forestall?

For high and holy ends God made her strong,
  And set her on the sacred heights of trust,
The constant foe of wrong.
Her forces unto Righteousness belong,
  That prostrate forms may rise from out the
    dust,
And sighing change to song.

Never shall she forget, as years speed on,
  That unto God her virgin troth was given ;
That 'neath His benison
The mighty triumphs of her past were won ;
  And so for her the stars shall strive from
    Heaven,
If righteous deeds be done.

Columbia enthronèd ; through all time
   Swift answering to Freedom; they who rose
For sake of her sublime,
Are pledge that ever, as the race shall climb
   Yet higher, she shall point to paths that
     close
Upon the ages' prime.

OUR SOLDIERS.

O SOLDIERS, who stood for the Flag of our
  Nation !
Columbia's children can never forget,
How you, through the grace of your sacred
  oblation,
Her honor and glory invincible set.

Behold the proud Banner of Liberty streaming!
  The Flag of our Union, the Red, White and
  Blue !
Its Stripes all undimmed and its Stars ever
  beaming,
Baptized in the blood of the brave and the
  true.

You marched and were weary, you fought and
  were wounded,
  You fell in the battle, you sank in the storm ;
But out of your sacrifice Heaven has rounded
  The hope of the ages to beauteous form.

Across the scarred fields of your struggles im-
  mortal,
  In rev'rent reviewing the hosts of the free
Shall trace the red paths which you trod to
  Fame's portal,
  And sacredly pledge through the years that
  will be,

To follow unswerving your feet of devotion,
  Inspired by your holy and generous deeds ;

And filled with a pure and a patriot emotion,
  Be true in their Country's imperative needs.

Upon the firm granite the marvellous story
  Of valor, with chisel of love, is engraved ;
The ages shall read, and exalt to new glory
  The crimson-stained banner you gallantly
    saved.

Around the green mounds where your forms
    lie a-sleeping,
  The People shall gather again and again ;
And, blessing your memories, place in your
    keeping
  The palms of thanksgiving, the laurels of
    pain.

All quickened by Duty's ensanguined libation,
  A Nation's new flower has bloomed from the
    clay ;
The sweet asphodel of a fresh consecration,
  Sprung out of the graves of the Blue and the
    Gray.

Pass on, O our Soldiers, to heavenly capture !
  We follow swift after beneath your renown ;
Pass on to the bivouac of rest and of rapture !
  Behind you our freedom, before you your
    crown.

The Land of Promise.

.

THE LAND OF PROMISE.

THE mists on the mountain peaks
  Melt fleet in the glad new morn;
  The hope of the world is born;
The Sphinx of the ages speaks.

The wrinkled forehead of Time
  Responds to his laughing soul;
  The runner has reached the goal;
And all things fall into rhyme.

The winds are poets, and sing
    September back into June ;
    The radiant asters swoon,
All purpling toward the Spring.

The bitter is changed to sweet ;
    The bruises of battle heal ;
    And Peace stands again at the wheel,
And turns it with glowing feet.

O God-given Occident!
    O Land of Promise ! whose sphere
    Is Nature's enlarged career
And Spirit's divine ascent ;

Reserved for the fulness of days
   Through haze of the desert past!
   A Canaan revealed at last
Of fruited and flowered ways!

From sea to the granite hills,
   From crests of snow to the sea,
   Rush, flashing with energy,
Innumerous crystal rills.

The mountains impatient stand
   For mystic call of desire;
   The vales inviting conspire
For magic touch of command;

Expectant of labor's keys,
   Strong-wrought at the forge of hope,
   Their subterrene doors to ope,
Disclosing earth's treasuries;

Great inner chambers of gold,
   And vaults of potential heat,
   Primeval power's retreat,
The store of the ages old;

The store of the ages new,
   And force for the higher trend,
   Where Nature and Spirit blend
In rise toward the blazoned blue.

Fair Land from the sea to the sea
Awaiting the great To-be!

Fulfilment of Liberty's dream,
The voice of the People supreme!

The throne of Justice secure,
The rights of man to endure!

The home of the world's oppressed,
The earth's great hearthstone of rest!

All barriers broken down,
And every man with a crown !

One Union never to fall !
One Flag afloat over all !

THE END.

www.ingramcontent.com/pod-product-compliance
Lightning Source LLC
Chambersburg PA
CBHW030627270326
41927CB00007B/1338